Salty Lemon

Salty Lemon

journey from salty to sweet

Rachel Laymoun

Rachel Laymoun

Dedication

This book is dedicated to Beezy.

Most of it was written in your home...or crying in a hammock on your deck. You loved me & my lil one during this time like no other. The gentle, patient, kind, unconditional love you showed me kept the lights on. Your quiet love kept me going. If you loved me in my mess then I wanted to know what was so loveable about me. I kept looking till I found it for myself. You sat with me in my storm so I will always share my sunshine I found with you.

Love,
Rach

Preface

This book is about loving yourself through hard transitions. About learning the difference between the voice of fear & that of intuition. I wrote these poems while going through a divorce, but please understand that the pain processed on these pages goes beyond a marriage ending. Divorce was just the catalyst needed to force me to address all of the ways I was hiding from my true self. The father of my child is someone I will always be rooting for. I am grateful for what I learned about myself & life while by his side. I am now looking forward to how we will individually grow while walking the separate journey's meant for us.

8.4.20
Poetry
I will fill my home & my heart with it
I will not accept anything less than poetry
with words
with thoughts
with energy exchanging hugs
with positive glances
with sincere intention
with reflection of the impact
only poetry in

8.12.20
You knew
You ignored the knowing
It was an inconvenient truth
Bury it. Bend it. Break it.
Oh you tried
It doesn't go calmly...
The truth

It lingers like a toothache
seemingly gone till that
first cold sip
first touch of sugar
Pain so sharp & piercing
from the festering cavity
that grew deeper from neglect

More pain is the only path to heal
Drill out each infectious lie
Fill the hole with your pure knowing
Sit with the uncomfortable truth
Listen. Learn. Leave it be.

8.12.20-2
Pain is what tells us
where the wound is
It is not the wound itself
Follow it

Where does it hurt
How long has it hurt
What kind of hurt
The body keeps score
The body is attempting to tell the mind
Through pain

Follow the pain
Recognize it
Observe it
Feel it all
Then heal
But not a second before

8.13.20
Find peace in the pause
Breathe
Repeat their inquiry
Request clarity
Reiterate please
Rephrase for me
Reconcile variances

8.13.20-2
Stop talking
to others
Start writing
to yourself

Trust that you know
because you know
You've known for a while

8.18.20
Each day feels lighter
Tears fall so heavy
Over him. Over her.
Anxiety of anticipation
He doesn't back down
I retreat. I cower.
Ready to lick his wounds
Heal my own alone

But yet...lightness continues

Peace fills spaces in my soul
Where doubt retreats from

Peace is air
Doubt is concrete

She will be okay
I will be okay
One day at a time

9.1.20
Feel the feelings.

Name them & know them.

So when they visit you again that interaction is void of those first introduction jitters. Fear. Sadness. Joy. Excitement. Feelings are not good or bad, just as humans are not typically one or the other. They just ARE.

The one I keep trying to kick out is Anger. They are the one I am most fearful of, because I never know who is coming with them. I don't know what they will leave behind for me to clean up. What relationships will need mending after their uninvited stay?

I admit...I am not being fair to Anger. Anger has made me brave. Anger has been a shield when fear came sharp as a knife. It was buoyancy when sadness flooded in. It was a quiet reminder of the truth when joy clouded my memory.

I will reconcile with Anger.

I will let it be.

9.8.20
When the deep breaths flow easier
When the sleep comes faster
When the steps don't linger
When the thoughts don't freeze

The next stage of grief

9.9.20

Intent loses weight post execution
Transforming into air
Unseen in lungs...flowing through hair
Impact stays heavy like pollution
Heft of the earth under feet
Dirt soiled hands or flowers smelling sweet

9.9.20-2

Lies for manipulated compromise
Instant gratification
    for shallow validation
Soul left so hungry darling
Time to run free from charming

9.10.20-2

My ego leaves me hungry every time I feed her
An empty well never filling up
A bucket dropped never returning water for my soul
Yet here I stand again...tossing in my last dime

9.10.20-3
Words words words
A medium of the soul
A starting line of sorts
Cannot stand alone
Cannot heal the hurt
What follows is the antidote
For the sting of past choice
Speak up with intention
That goes beyond your voice

9.10.20-4
I will write with ink, not lead
Free the caged words inside my head

Not explanations pleading for validation
Only poetry intended for communication

9.10.20-5
Truth is bitter on the tongue
But nourishing to the soul
Lies so sweet & beautiful
The empty swallow whole

9.11.20
Vengeance doesn't mend a heart that's broken
Disregard all ignorant words spoken

Why put your name on tips of sharp tongues?
Save your peace, keep that breath in your lungs

Deaf ears require miracles to hear

9.12.20
The timing of your love gets me through
Boundaries set so my pain doesn't drown you
Your empathy is admirable but self love more so
Wishing & wanting for your ability to let go
Each dark night of the soul I see more of your face
I know it's because I've finally learned grace

9.12.20-2
Deep breaths
Inhale
Exhale
Press on
One step
Then another
I will be softer than my mother

9.16.20
Such a pleasant distraction
Those sensual interactions
Swiftly pain clears my head
The second I lay on your bed
Grateful for a moment to breathe
A vacation from my grief

9.16.20-3
Having trouble catching my breath
pain sitting heavy on my chest
don't cry now rach, not here
get back to work
get back to the mask
behind this mask they can't see
my lips clenched tight
to keep the rest of my face sitting right
man...this is gonna be a long ride

9.16.20-4
grief sitting heavy today
at work fighting tears
take note of the feelings
guilt. sadness. anger. fear.
you can do this...hold it together
reconcile cash. confirm contracts.
focus on what you can control
dismiss lies & amplify facts

LIE - it's all your fault
& you deserve to suffer
FACT - blame is equally shared
& you're a great mother

9.17.20
Scroll scroll scroll
Swipe swipe swipe
Keep the pain at bay
I can't feel. I can't write.
I can't cry. I can't speak.
I'll deflect the easy way
Disassociate
Get through today

9.24.20
Know my place
In your bed
Give you space
In your head
Save my words
Already spoken
Can't be heard
Heart still broken

10.4.20
Breathe into the ache
Fill the space pain resides
Air & peace over doubt
Push it out
That heavy lie
Spoken over you like a curse
But those are not your words
Not your truth
You get to choose
What has power over you

10.4.20-2
Too much
Full & vibrant
Saucey & strong
A bite in her words, yes
But they flow like a song

Too much
Loud & stern
Sarcastic & bright
She knows she makes you squint
But she won't dim her light

Subtle yet abrasive
Elusive but persuasive

Too much?
She's just getting started

10.8.20
Sad but grateful
In pain yet at peace
Somber & beautiful
Sweet soul release

10.8.20-2
I walk with fear but forward I go
Intuition leading & thus I'll grow
I know I'll make it; I know we'll rise
I know now that fear tells lies

10.14.20
Here I lay
Minutes from midnight
Feeling the pain of divorce
The uncertainty of my future
My dreams laced with pain
My dreams changing again
Dreams that wake me in the night
Every single night
With a gasp
Or with a tear
It's okay
It's okay to lean in
It's okay to zone out
Just be honest either way
When the questions come about
Honest with yourself, not them
The inward monologue
Keep that true
Outward dialogue
Just make it through
Lay at midnight & open your soul
Let it flow free & wild
Don't plan
Don't project
Float. Flow. Feel.
Don't subject yourself
To the pressures previously placed
Creating a new standard
A new regular
True & beautiful space

10.15.20
Speak it out
As a blessing
As a hope
As a desire
As a declaration
As if it is already mine

I am worthy
Worthy of reciprocated energy
Worthy to have grace returned
Worthy of the love I give

Accountability over expectation
Partnership over parenthood
Communication over manipulation
Vulnerability over insecurity

My mind their coffee shop
Where we share ideas to save us all
My body their gym
Where we cum together to work out pain
My heart their safe home
But one that is shared in how it's cared for
My spirit their resting place
But I have equal access to peace in theirs

Oh what a beautiful love I am worthy of

10.16.20
The breaking
The healing
The growing

The shaking
The kneeling
The knowing

The aching
The reeling
The flowing

This is how we begin again
This is how we settle in
This is how we love ourselves
This is how she found herself

10.16.20-2
It will put food in her mouth
It will buy her next house
It will settle the soul long fraught
It will filter harmful lessons taught

Write

10.16.20-3
freedom found between syllables
she doesn't have a plan
this time the flow will carry her
anxiety rises but falls
this time she falls with it
the floating
the rising
the falling
like breath in her lungs
the peace in her soul
these words incomplete
but heart finally whole
no longer half of another
a vessel mended with gold
filled to the brim
begin again
her story will be told

10.18.20
Volume up
Blood pumping
Nerves on edge
Heart jumping
Triggered
Where's the exit
Where's the keys
Instant replay again
Curse my memories

10.22.20
Your mind ain't broke cuz it's running
Give yourself grace as you enter this becoming
Surround yourself with real, only real
Immerse yourself in others that know how to feel

10.25.20
The love I yearn for so deeply already exists within me
The company I desire is available inside my own mind
The comfort I have sought out in others is present within
my heart
The energy exchanges I chase are beautiful, but my spirit is
already radiating energy that I can soak in

You are enough
You are abundant
How beautiful you are

10.23.20
Eleven days sober of pleasant distractions
With a clear mind I'm replaying interactions
Conversations long ended but very much alive
Frustrations have me winded, mind in overdrive

Float. Flow. Feel. Free.
That's the goal here Rach...Don't forget
He didn't. WANT. ME.
Lie or truth.... irrelevant.
A sign you're not floating yet.

10.25.20
Thirteen days sober of pleasant distractions
Retrospect the filter of past actions
Lessons, not mistakes, learned from impatience
Forgiveness & self-compassion commence

10.27.20
Fifteen days sober of deflection & booze
Somber enough to let loneliness be my muse
I gave into flirtation & it didn't scratch the itch
Back to full-fledged inner work before I flip a switch

10.28.20
Currently uncomfortable with that itchy feeling
The one you get when a wound is healing
It's that skin pulled tight not quite right
Keep you up at night searching for a light
Kinda feeling

You see...I made some decisions
Executed some much needed revisions
But often the right thing makes your ears ring
With the kind of pain that pulsates through
With those head to toe shivers that imbue
Sitting heavy with this pain down the spine
Or in that one spot you can't reach in your mind
You squirm in discontent like a child told no
Maybe if you sit still you'll learn to let go
Instead I jump up, jump out cuz I think I know
Know better than the victims before me
Assuming I'm seeing things they didn't see
Somehow privy to knowledge of lessons unlearned
Clearly setting myself up to get burned
Like a house plant left in the sun at noon
Not used to midday rays, becoming thirsty soon
Losing half its leaves due to its arrogant heart
Wanted a taste of the warmth but was left parched
Stages to this process but I'm impatient as fuck
I don't know if I can wait on good luck

11.2.20
My mother named me after Rachel from the bible
A woman whose love life is a complicated time table
Quickly enthralled...Jacob vowed to work 7 years for her hand
As if this would somehow make me understand
Understand my worth in the eyes of my mother
As she told me to wait to find another lover
Then on their wedding night he was given her sister instead
So 7 more years Rachel waited to be wed
"But oh how much Jacob adored her!
For he broke his back for 14 years to earn her"
My mother exclaimed as I signed for my divorce
As if this story holds relevance to my current course
My heart broken & hungry for love again
Am I subject to 14 years of waiting to begin?

11.3.20
The first time I was touched it burned
His skin like a torch to tissue paper
Like a tree scorched & then healed over
No ash or visible damage present
The years that followed I grew
Without memory of the singed bark
Long layered over with new growth
A decade of touches commenced
Most like sandpaper but sometimes sunshine
Rings growing tighter together from drought
Reaching for the light I stretched thin
Roots dug down in search of water not found
Withering away that first touch started to burn
The charcoal within an unscratchable itch
Chop it down. Damage shown
From here new growth will churn

11.4.20
Your heartbeat once in sync with mine
Tiny movements that swayed with my hips
Perfect soul radiating from within me
Never wanting to share you but knowing
Your light would illuminate this world

11.4.20-2
You are my sunshine
The light in my darkest nights
Depression remedy

11.5.20

On behalf of the ones who walked away
No cups of hot tea & warm hugs await us
Seen as the hands that dropped the glass
Shattered & scattered in the home you made
You're the broom & the floor
No one feels empathy for the broom
Just the glass now broken
No one gives hugs to the floor
Just mourns the shards in the trash
As if we won't be picking bloody bits from our toes alone
Finding those tiny knives in bare feet for weeks
Guilt weighing heavier than the liquid spilt
Slippery palms & hard feelings
Clean it up the best that you can
Cuz you can be hurt & healed by your own hands

11.6.20
An ode to my daughter, her spirit pure & strong
She exudes authenticity, like a bird sings its song
Her smile could cut diamonds
Her laugh heal a broken spirit
Her touch soul food & I long to be near it

11.16.20

The times I want to text you
When fear & lonely crash together
Like toddlers in a running hug
But void of that joy & laughter
When the tears fall heavy
Like a coffee cup overfilled
Burning & staining my skin
Thumbs moving fast for a fix
Heart says it won't scratch the itch
When anxiety crawls up my spine
Like a roach on your wall at night
You can feel it but don't dare turn on a light

The times I want to text you
Not when my cup is full
Not when my worth is known
Not when my self love imbues
My number known but never used
That tells me all I need to know
Strongly implies to let you go
Infatuation still flows like a levee breached
So each act of self control like
a sand bag to a leak
Purpose served & lesson learned
No reason to let these tears burn
Let them fall like rain &
drench my thirsty heart
Let new growth sprout & admire it like art

The times I want to text you
A signal to go deeper within
To not mourn what has ended
but start to begin again
Find a new path in my mind
to answers ever present
Like a traveler with no destination
but knows their next step
I will find my way back to myself
Words from another cannot guide me
somewhere they have never been

The times I want to text you
Will reduce in frequency as time goes on
Each moment heavy in the present
But it passes like a workout completed
Oxytocin your reward for giving
your body what it needed

11.18.20

It's the audience that keeps you safe

11.20.20
An ode to my daughter
She is like sunshine at midnight
Warm on your skin
Too much to stare directly at
Filled to the brim with light

Rays bringing life at light speed
Growth springing forth
An unwieldy force at work
She is everything we need

She is like rain after a drought
Pure & gentle but all encompassing
Quenching that which withered away
Bringing hope in place of doubt

Washing away the settled dust
Drops taking dirt back to earth
Again she rises to rinse again
Weak spots exposed turning to rust

She is like a harvest moon
Diffused light shone on your soul
Soft revelations seen
The tide, me...she keeps in tune

Providing sight in the dark
Calm & cool but just enough
A little extra time for the work
She is my midnight spark

11.29.20
What do they touch that I can't reach?
I've got a hunch God's got a lesson to teach
Finger tips across skin dopamine flowing again
Light squeeze gentle kiss shirts off pants amiss
Mouth hungry hands exploring
Swelling where my tongue is touring

Imagine if I explored myself this way
Poured enthusiasm into chasing my pleasure
Praised my body just for showing up & being ready to play
What shame is still attached to oxytocin to be severed?
I love the way my thighs feel both strong & soft
My hands can grab a hold & find comfort in both
I love the dimples on all four cheeks plus my chin
Little dips to let love pour in
The way my eyes crease when my smile pulls tight
The way the line between my brows deepen when I squint in the light
I love how quickly my mind lands on a sarcastic rebuttal with no trouble
I am beautiful in both body & mind
My words sweet like honey but sometimes hot sauce
My love falls heavy but needed like a post draught storm
Hugs, warm but light like an April sweater
Never know what I'll give you like Louisiana weather
I love the way I fail because it's always a new show
Mistakes not repeated as I learn & grow
Write it all down, especially the ugly
Choosing an authentic life is what makes me so lovely

12.3.20

I'm not carrying it, so I can't tell you how heavy it is.
Emotional weight.

12.14.20
Don't give me a drink
No matter how thirsty I appear
I will rot from the bottom
No matter your intentions dear
Wait until I've shrunken down
Roots reaching through the dirt
Searching out what is left
Wait to help so you don't hurt
Water me now & I'll freeze
Cold nights have arrived
Fill me now & you'll see
Death will be your surprise

1.30.21

Searching for something lost in this house leaves me lost in time

Where is the last place I had it.... My peace of mind

I don't really know where to start with this mess

But I know a clean house can alleviate stress

I look at that pile of trauma lumped with soul food

I'll sort that out later when I'm more subdued

A sink full of dirty wishes & cloudy water

Save that for when I'm feeling smarter

I can't fathom filtering faith from fear

He heaved his hefty hate in the hallways here

But he's not a bad man, just raised on bad love

I've just done all I can to help him rise above

In this house, the guest room holds our mommy issues

We've kept it stocked like good host full of tears & tissues

His mother made this bed with unverbalized affection

Throw pillows carefully placed gave me the appearance of connection

Messy dresser drawers filled the same way her son loved me, careless & rushed

He had been clothed in a bitter Mother's roughness & then deprived of her touch

So, he had never known the comfort of cotton

The warm cozy feeling of not being forgotten

Whereas my matriarchal muse placed pallets of poetry for Sunday morning snuggles

My mother's love kept us warm despite the chill of her struggles

But like hers before her, my mama modeled giving till you're empty

So, I gave him all I had no matter what it did to me

Down the hall there's a closet where we placed our patriarchal pain
Its door hiding our father's fuckups with hinges strained
Shoved onto these shelves are our blankets of insecurity
I swapped mine for one woven of self love's surety
Layered in these layers of linens are things I've never seen
Like the reasons for your rage & other things obscene
My memories of violent altercations are folded neatly, top shelf
Years of therapy to unpack them & then organize myself
You never had to fold your daddy issues to fit in my arms
But maybe if I had made you, you would have caused less harm
Instead, I left this crowded closet to be stuffed to the brim
Just long enough for you to start acting like him
A jar of jealousy juxtaposed against Jesus & the juices
Our fridge reeks of false narratives that rendered us cold & ruthless
We followed family recipes not knowing there was better
Fed each other lunches of lies & called it love letters
Your cheesy lines have molded...me into a mess of stress
A twisted noodle bowl soul that you weren't ready to digest
Behind the leftover good intentions, I put my intuition in the freezer
There fear is kept fresh on ice should I ever need her
Pantry stocked still with the kind of food that makes you ill
Cases of cookies next to boxes of bitterness
Our bodies were starved of true love's tenderness
I couldn't cook up peace in this kitchen if I tried
& I'm so sorry for the trust I spoiled when I lied
We may not agree on how it got here but...
Divorce is what's for dinner dear

1.23.21
3 wishes for my daughter

1. I wish that you feel the depth of my love when I wear your tears like lip gloss. My love is deep enough to keep you afloat through any loss. It is resilient to withstand your tantrums, your attitude, & now 50% of the time...your absence. This love is interwoven into my skin. It gave birth to your soul & to mine a new facet.

2. I wish for you to love yourself as much as you do chocolate milk & Cheetos. For you to know your desires & feel safe to voice them wherever we go. Self-love will feed & protect you when fear & doubt start their monologues in your tiny mind. We do positive affirmations for this reason to keep that inner voice of yours speaking kind

3. I wish for you love & be loved in the beautiful way that healed people do it. Finding someone that you can give & take energy from in balance to get through it. I hope for you to fall & feel everything beautiful about love on this journey. I know because I loved you truly madly deeply first, I really don't have to worry

www.ingramcontent.com/pod-product-compliance
Lightning Source LLC
Chambersburg PA
CBHW061718130726
47996CB00006B/2385